# Autism and Angels
## By Claire Marsh

To Harvey for showing me the way,
and my illustrator Evie.

# Contents

Introduction- This Is My True Story     7

Welcoming Harvey Into The World     9

Harvey's Struggle     14

Unexplained Events Growing Up     16

Harvey's Poor Sleep Pattern     20

My Back Pain     23

Harvey Gets Really Sick     25

Summer Holiday 2011     32

Meeting a Healer     39

Alex Gone Fishing     43

My Pre-Op     45

I Get a sign     49

EFT     51

Taking My First Degree Reiki     52

Four Leaf Clover     55

Harvey's Friend     57

A Year On     59

How Can You Change Your Life Now     62

## Introduction-

## This Is My True Story

I have lived 39 years for the here and now, rushing to achieve work and family commitments, always being unlucky, and meeting misfortune. This all came to a climax in the summer of 2011, after having a horrific encounter of abuse, when I was at my lowest, fearing the worst for my poorly son with special needs. My back pain was intolerable.

Then something magical happened. Its almost as if I have lived in a dark room all my life, with the door bolted shut. Harvey my beautiful son with Downs Syndrome, has shown me how to unlock that door. Its like walking into a brightly lit room that has been there all the time, but I would never have entered it without his help. The world of Angels and Love.

No really you need to read on, it has transformed my life. Caring for a needy person is immensely hard, and if I can help one other person with my story, then I feel I have fulfilled my life's purpose.

To get as many people to cross the divide from non-spiritual to spiritual is my ultimate goal.

It has been a long voyage of discovery, and I understand that it may not sound believable. If you are sceptical, I hope it will put a question of intrigue in you mind and initiate your own journey.

After school I trained for 7 years at College in Architecture and Civil Engineering, but then the children came along, so I embarked on a new chapter.

# Welcoming Harvey into the world

I have always lived for the here and now. Growing up, expecting a scientific answer and reason for everything. My perception of life has changed in the last year, and I just felt I needed to share this.

We are not alone, and you don't need to feel this anymore.

If you are caring for a needy person, life gets challenging, and lonely.

There has been a long string of events that has led me to this point. But mostly it is down to my beautiful son Harvey, who has downs syndrome and "pockets of autism" as the so called specialist put it.

He was born 9 years ago on the 23rd July 2003. My pregnancy had been pretty straight forward, so when I went into labour, I wasn't expecting what was to unfold that night. During labour, I became very tired and suddenly found myself looking down at my body from the ceiling, and watching the midwife shouting, "Claire, wake up, that's enough gas and air!"

I was thinking, I can't go now, I need to be down there with my lovely husband Alex and my children.

When Harvey finally slithered out, he was like jelly, and ginger! I already had a 5 year old son Myles, so I remember feeling a bit deflated, as I was desperate for a daughter. At the time I thought his difference in muscle tone was due to the fact the I had a different husband from my first sons dad.

Initially it all seemed fine, and I had a bath with Harvey, and then was settled into bed with him. I thought I would have a go at breast feeding. I had bottle fed Myles, as I had been too vain to give up my figure, but now I was 31 and knew Alex would love me no matter what I looked like.

Harvey couldn't suck, as he was tired, so I placed him in his cot by my bed for a nap. The midwife came in to take a standard sugar level test, but this indicated that his levels had dropped dramatically. He was slipping into a coma. Another midwife was buzzed, and rushed in. He was wrapped in a foil blanket, and we were put in an ambulance, as we were only at a maternity unit. Harvey had gone unconscious.

As the ambulance sped off, I was clutching Harvey in his little foil blanket, thinking what's going on? Suddenly the bed slid into the back doors of the ambulance. In the haste, the bed had not been clipped down, and I nearly dropped Harvey.

Alex followed in our car behind. Afterwards he said he was terrified as the blue light was flashing, and he didn't know if he could keep up with the speed the ambulance was going.

When we arrived at Exeter Hospital, Harvey was put in the premature baby unit in a hot cot, and Alex and I were put in a room off the corridor to the maternity canteen. Time stopped - we had no answers. I just wanted to be with my baby. Would I see him again alive? That was a long night, it felt like it couldn't be happening, a blank nothingness.
At 9 o'clock, I asked if it would be ok to make a few phone calls, so I went to the phone booth and rang my mum and sisters to explain what had happened.

At that point a midwife tapped me on the shoulder, and said, "the doctors waiting in your room, and you need to go back."
I sat on the bed with Alex. The doctor had an assistant. He simply said, "We believe your baby has downs syndrome."

I remember blurting out, "but they don't live very long?"
He replied, "They can live up to their 50's."
I said, "That's not long, I will out live him!"
Then the crying started.

We asked if we could see him. I put a little woolly hat on
Harvey's head, and picked him up. At that point, he didn't
have a name, as we were going to call him Joe, but that
didn't seem right now.
As I cradled him in my hands, I thought, how am I going
to be able to do this? And Harvey did this large sigh,
then seemed to stop breathing.
I looked at Alex, and he looked at me. A few seconds
later, Harvey breathed again, and I started to cry. Alex
said, "its ok. I know what your were thinking, I was
thinking it too!"
Basically, I had almost felt relieved that he had stopped
breathing, but as soon as he gasped, I had then felt so
guilty feeling that way. I knew we were going to treasure
every moment with Harvey, and we would give him the
best go at life we could!

When we left the Hospital, with Harvey, the midwife
gave me this print out:-

*Holland?!?" you say. "What do you mean Holland?? I signed up for Italy! I'm supposed to be in Italy. All my life I've dreamed of going to Italy."*

*But everyone you know is busy coming and going from Italy... and they're all bragging about what a wonderful time they had there. And for the rest of your life, you will say "Yes, that's where I was supposed to go. That's what I had planned."*

*But... if you spend your life mourning the fact that you didn't get to Italy, you may never be free to enjoy the very special, the very lovely things ... about Holland.*

It still makes me cry today when I read it, but it is so true. I never imagined the things in life Harvey would be capable of showing me, and I am now so glad we did end up in Holland after all!

# Harvey's Struggle

The early years were an immense struggle. We were given mountains of literature to read, and told every child with downs syndrome is different in how they are affected. Initially we thought he had mosaic downs, which means only a bit of him might have downs syndrome. But when the blood results came back, he had the non inherited downs syndrome.

Harvey has a low immunity and has suffered a lot with illness. He has been admitted to hospital lots of times with chest infections, collapsed lungs, pneumonia, kidney infections, croup, and the last time it was suspected meningitis, but it turned out to be strep A infection.

He has had to struggle all the way along. Initially we felt he was immensely bright, this ability to learn has been held back by all the illness.

When he was 2, he could say words like, "mum", "dad", "duck", "one" and "two". But this then all stopped after he had his MMR injection. He was really poorly from it, and developed a measles rash and temperature. His speech then stopped.

He has had two lots of eye ducts surgery to help prevent his eyes weeping and becoming sticky and infected, but this didn't work.

He had his tonsils and adenoids removed at the age of 3, as his tonsils were constantly infected and extremely large, which restricted his ability to breath at night and swallow food. He found it difficult to chew as his muscles are weak in his jaw, and he was frightened of chocking. Feeding Harvey has always been a challenge, and I would say, this had been the most difficult and frustrating part of Harvey.

You have to fight all the way along for the support you so desperately need. It took us three attempts to claim Disability allowance. It's only through meeting other parents in the same boat that your find out about any help out there.

## Unexplained Events Growing Up.

When I was growing up, my parents built a bungalow on the grounds of an old chapel and grave yard. There were no signs that it had been a grave yard though, except we did find a couple of grave stones in field gateways near by.

When my dad dug the footings and drains for the bungalow, he said he dug through some graves, but I never saw them.

My bedroom was the end bedroom, at night my chest of draws would start to tick. I would call my mum, and she would come in, really crabby that I had dragged her away from her sit down. (I totally understand this now I have children!). She would say, "don't be silly, draws don't tick!" As I laid there in the night, I would hear the ticking, and with my eyes shut, I could see a man in a uniform charging on a horse in a rush. I didn't sense a bad feeling, just urgency.

One night my mum did hear the ticking, so she researched a logical explanation for this. Her conclusion was that the mites that live in wood, all bang their bums in unison on occasions for some reason! And that was the factual answer.

I kind of went with this, as it sort of made me less scared, but it did concern me that my chest of draws were full of disgusting insect mites so minute I couldn't see them!

I put this all to the back of my mind until 2 years ago, when I was at my local swimming pool in the changing rooms. I happened to get talking to another lady changing. I don't know why we started talking, but it turned out that she lived at my old house where I had grown up. She mentioned that her daughter who was 3, was having trouble sleeping. I asked why, and she said "she says she has a solider on a horse in her room at night!"

I asked what bedroom, and it was my old bedroom. I was amazed. It hadn't all been my imagination. I then told her that I used to see a man in a uniform on a horse, and not to doubt her daughter. I think when your parents don't believe you, it has a knock on your confidence.

When I was about 20, I was with a group of my boyfriends friends in a hotel, and they had all decided to do a Ouija board. I didn't agree with this, as my mum had said they were dangerous, and it was all mind games. When I turned up they had written the alphabet on bits of torn paper, and placed them in a circle on the table, with a upside down glass in the middle.

I sat down at the table next to my boyfriend thinking, what harm can it do, when they asked me to place my finger on the glass. After all its all a pile of tosh!

I was slightly shocked when once I placed my finger on the glass, along with everyone else, my arm was yanked by the glass. (My finger was only hovering over it, there was nothing connecting my finger physically to the glass). The glass started to spell out my name, and I forced my arm away from the glass, completely petrified! There was only one other persons finger that had stayed on the glass, and that lady wasn't holding me in any way either. I didn't sleep that night, I couldn't understand what had gone on. I didn't do that again!

The only other slightly spiritual thing I have ever done, was once in a pub, when I was about 24. A friend of a friend was telling me she could read palms. So I said, "alright then, what does my hand say?"

She looked at my hand and said, "On the birth of my second child, my destiny would change!" then she pushed my hand away and wouldn't say any more, as she looked worried. I thought, oh great, I'm going to die in child birth!! But oh well its all a load of baloney! But deep down it kind of worried me. Hence when I came out of my body when I was in labour with Harvey, I did think at that point she had been right. In a funny way she was right, as my destiny did change when I had Harvey.

## Harvey's Poor Sleep Pattern

Harvey needs constant cuddles and reassurance that your there. He wakes all through the night, wanting a cuddle to settle. As he has been so unwell, its hard for us to break this habit. We have tried so many different types of sleep programmers. The putting back to bed was the worst, as we spent all night putting him back and walking away. In the end after a couple of weeks, and sore backs, we just laid down next to him again. His crying develops throat infections and croup.

We started to feel that someone or something was waking him, as he would sit bolt upright in bed and start babbling. Or rush over to the window and stare and babble at the nights sky. It was as if he could see some thing we couldn't. Then one morning about 4 years ago, Harvey, my daughter Evie who was 2 at the time and myself, were sitting in bed, and I was reading a story to them, when a shadow went across the room. I thought nothing of it, but Evie asked "Mummy, why did that boy just walk through the room?"

Harvey was smiling to as if he had seen an old friend. Stupidly I said in my naivety, "that was just a shadow from the sun and clouds outside darling, that wasn't a boy."

I think the doubt I installed into Evie that day, closed her perception of anything spiritual. As Harvey didn't understand what I was saying, it didn't effect him!

Now I started to think more about what Harvey might be seeing, and this started to escalate when one night Harvey was sat on the toilet with a poorly tummy, where he had been sitting for quite some time. I was gently rubbing his tummy. He looked up and signed to me. (He uses makaton sign language , as he wears a hearing aid, and he finds it too hard to speak). He signed "lady" and "wings". I said "what, butterfly, moth?"
He sign "no". He did it again and signed "lady" and "wings". When I said angel, he signed yes, and was really happy with me.

This did make my skin crawl up my neck to the top of my head. It was completely out of my comprehension or understanding.

Shortly afterwards, I took my children to the 'Big Sheep', which is a ball pit  style activity place. It was a meeting set up by the local Downs syndrome association, about 1 hours drive from home. I was casually talking to another parent of a child with downs syndrome, while my kids were rushing around. I thought I'm going to have to ask, and I hope the lady doesn't think I'm bonkers. So I said "the other night, when Harvey was poorly, he told me he could see an angel."
She replied, "oh that's quite common, downs syndrome children often say that when they are unwell."

I was over the moon. I had reassurance that I wasn't mad. It wasn't sleep deprivation that was making me start to believe in angels.
The thing with Harvey is, he lives for here and now, you cant say to him we are going on holiday tomorrow, or its your birthday tomorrow, as he will expect it to happen there and then, so this is why if Harvey says there's a lady with wings, then he is definitely seeing a lady with wings!!

# My Back Pain

Obviously the stresses and strains of bringing up a family is hard work for any one, but Harvey and his challenging behaviour, needing 1 to 1 at all times, to prevent him harming himself or others, is extremely mentally draining, along with the poor sleep pattern.

There is no let up, my life is action packed. I have always had a weakness in my lower back, I think I like to be a busy person, and Harvey needs constant lifting and restraint, which doesn't help my lower back pain. Last year the pain escalated to the point where I was seeing a physiotherapist through my doctors referral, which took 6 months to initiate. The physiotherapist, after about 3 months of treatment, referred me to hospital to have an MRI scan., as I explained the pain was excruciating.

I was wearing a tens machine all day and night at a level 5 or 6 some times. The MRI showed I had a herniated disc, this was trapping nerves in my leg causing pain all down it in my thigh, calf and foot. The pain would get worse through the day and I was taking Ibuprofen, Paracetamol, and diclopfenac, to the max I could take.

It was suggested to me by a friend that it might be worth going to see a chiropractor. So I made an appointment with one. It cost 45 pounds for a half hour appointment, where he wiggled me about a bit, and then said it would get better if I pushed myself a bit more, and did more exercise. Well this was really hurtful. I walked 2 miles a day with my dogs, and swam 64 lengths twice a week, on top of running around like a headless chicken after Harvey. He also said if I lost a stone, it would help. He was looking at my chest when he said that. As I was anorexic when I was younger, I have always been obsessed with sport, and my husband tells me I have a lovely figure. He knew I would worry about what the man had said, and told me to take no notice. When I told my friend who had passed on the details of the chiropractor, she also told me that I shouldn't get any thinner. This lady used to 1 to 1 Harvey for me once every 3 weeks on a Sunday morning, but she found it too difficult, and said Harvey really needs 2 adults to support him when out and about as she found it too much.

# Harvey Gets Really Sick

Probably the lowest point we got to in Harvey's health was May 2011. He became really poorly during a Tabloid paper weekend break, to a holiday site. We had been swimming every day and on the Sunday he became sick. By the Monday, he was really unwell with bloodshot eyes and a red line tracking down his face from his eyes. His ears were sore, and there was a start of a rash on his body. We took him to the doctor and he prescribed antibiotics, but getting any medicine into Harvey is impossible, as he spits it out at you. We administer pain killers through suppositories, as this was the only way we could help, but antibiotic suppositories are not licensed in the UK. (This does need to be licensed)

The next day happened to be his annual Pediatrics appointment, at the local hospital. We took him in and they took one look at him and sent him to the District hospital. The red rash had got worse, and they suspected he had meningitis.

The whole ordeal was horrendous.

By this point, due to the fact that we were living on the minimal amount of sleep anyway, when Harvey gets unwell, the chance of sleep gets even more challenging, as he is too restless. There is no reserve to fall back on.

The nurse was trying to put a canular into Harvey's arm, so they could administer IV antibiotics, and they needed to take bloods. My 7 year old Harvey was being held by Alex in a vice like grip to help the nurse and doctor. I was dangling funny toys at Harvey to distract him, but Harvey obviously feeling extremely unwell, was having none of it, thrashing about crying. The emotional stain of the whole situation on top of the room being incredibly hot, was too much for my husband Alex, and he said, "I'm going!" as he fell to the bed unconscious.

I grabbed Harvey so he didn't hit the floor. This was immensely difficult for me as my back hurt so bad, and I was supposed to avoid lifting. Harvey weighed 36Kg at that point. The bloods spilled out of Harvey's arm and all over the floor.

I looked at Alex lying there and thought, how am I going to cope if anything happens to you. He did come round, as he had just fainted, but the whole situation was too much.

After 3 days of Harvey receiving antibiotics , he picked right up, and the results came back that he didn't have meningitis, just a Strep A infection. This had caused the blood poising line on his face, both ears to perforate, and his throat infection. It had been frightening to watch how quickly the infection had took hold.

They needed to administer antibiotics for a further 10 days, but he was now feeling better, he was on the move again, and it was hard to keep him still and amused in his room. When the nurse was administering some drugs into his IV drip, I asked if the medicine was going into the wrong place into his arm, what would happen? She said a big blister would appear under the skin and it would sting him. I asked this because he was screaming in pain. I pointed out to the nurse that there was a big 1 $\frac{1}{2}$ inch blister appearing on his arm, and she immediately removed the canular. Well this was a disaster. All the struggle we had had to put the thing in, in the first place had been a nightmare. They knew they couldn't put Harvey through that again, so they said they could give him 1 off injections into his upper thigh every day instead. (Wouldn't suppositories have been easier!)

As it was getting difficult to keep him in the room, and to avoid catching anything, they were happy to let us go home, returning every day to have the injections.

Before we went, Harvey had to have the injection. It turn out due to his size, he would need 2 injections each time in either leg, and not at the same time. one after the other. They were the 1-2mm dia needles. I was worried it might effect Alex again, so I held Harvey and told him to look a away, but he could still hear the screaming.

When we were on our way home that day, which is an hour away, I said to Alex, shall we get Harvey a McDonalds? This is a kind of treat thing we do for Harvey when he has a hospital visit. At that point, we were going to have to take him back every day for the next 5 days and have him injected over and over.

Alex parked the car in the McDonalds car park, and I ran in to buy Harvey's burger and drink. After paying I stood to the side of the till, I thought out of the way, against the wall. I was just day dreaming about the past few days. It was really busy, and there wasn't much space to move. A young man was paying for his burger with a card. He looked at me and said, "Stop looking at my pin!"

I didn't say anything at first, and just shifted to the side as far as I could go. But then something inside me said, "Claire, you weren't looking at his pin, stand up for yourself girl!"

So I simply said, "I wasn't looking at your pin." I felt in quite a matter of fact manor, trying to put his mind at rest.

**OMG,** I should not have said that.

He started ragging on at me using a lot of expletives like "you fuXXXXX, bitXX, you were looking at my pin! If your weren't on CCTV right now I would smash your fuXXXXX face in!!!"

I was exhausted and emotional, and just wanted my burger so I could go, so I replied, "Oh so your saying on CCTV that if I wasn't on CCTV you'd smash my face in!"

I probably did say this now with some emotion in my voice. The young man started to get really abusive at me. I then said, "Could you stop swearing, there are children in the queue!"

At this point the man continued to rant and was looking very threatening at me, then the boy serving behind the counter said, "If you both don't stop arguing, you will both have to be escorted of the premises!"

Well I just burst into tears, the youth who had been bullying me was still ranting, his mate was egging him on, and no one behind in the queue had stuck up for me, and now I was going to be escorted off the premises. I had been very badly verbally abused, and I was frightened that the 2 men shouting at me were going to attack me outside, as they had threatened.

A lady working in McDonalds appeared, and put her arm around me and obviously had read the situation a bit better, she said "What was your order love?"

I said, "I cant remember." but she sorted it out and did escort me to the car. By this point I was crying uncontrollably and the phlegm and tears where covering my face.

Alex saw the state of me as I approached the car, and he had seen the 2 youths marched out of McDonalds, who were still hovering around the entrance looking menacing.

Alex shouted to me "What on earths the matter, what has gone on, is it to do with those lads?" and he pointed at the youths.

I said "Its nothing Alex, lets go home."

But he said "Right", and went marching over to the youths.

I could see a lot of pointing going on and they exchanged words. Then Alex marched into McDonalds and was demanding an explanation.

A couple that had been in the queue piped up and told Alex that I had been verbally attacked by the boys outside. Alex went back outside and started shouting at the youths again, saying "Do you know what me and my wife have just been through with our  son, I can assure you she isn't in the slightest bit interested in your pin!"

He replied "I couldn't give a shXX about your son!"

I could see this was getting out of control, so I started shouting out of the car window, "Please Alex, lets go home, Harvey needs more medicine!"

I felt like I was on a scene from some soap opera.

Alex retreated and as he approached the car, Harvey was signing to me he wanted his strawberry milkshake, but we didn't have any straws, and Harvey could only drink out of straws. Alex was very red faced when he got to the car, and the youths sloped off.

I said to Alex, "Love, Harvey wants a drink, and we haven't got a straw."

He looked at me and sighed, turned round and marched back into McDonalds.

Alex said everyone had been watching the commotion and stared at him as he walked in. I think they thought he was going to demand that he wanted the police. But he simply picked up 2 straws, and walked out again. He said he felt such a Berk!!

# Summer Holiday 2011

We went on holiday and stayed in a chalet on a holiday park. This holiday we won't forget!
There was Evie now 5, Harvey 8, Myles 13, Alex and myself in one chalet. My mum, her boyfriend Patrick, and my nanny in another. **The Holiday changed everything.**

When we walked into the chalet it had a negative sad feeling. I wanted to keep the curtains closed looking out at the bank in the bedroom. We were all woken up on the first morning by Alex screaming. Alex was sleeping in the double bedroom with Harvey, and I was sleeping in the childs bedroom with 3 single beds.
I asked Alex what he was screaming about and he said "oh nothing, just a stupid dream."

I didn't think any more about it until the next night. Everyone had gone to sleep, and I was lying there really getting quite frustrated that I needed to sleep, but my back was bad, and I was having to reset the Tens machine every 15 minutes as it only lasted that long. Alex said it was like listening to someone playing space invaders in the next room.

I heard this childs voice saying "Claire."
I looked around but both Myles and Evie lying next to me
were snoring, so I thought , oh my imagination. Then it
happened again. "Claire." said a childs voice. I was
watching both the children now, and it wasn't them!
Then it happened again. On the third chilling "Claire" I
ran into Alex's bedroom and woke him up.
I said "Has Harvey started to talk? A child is calling my
name."
Alex replied, "I'll tell you about it in the morning."
"About what?" I said.
"The same sort of thing happened to me last night." Alex
said.

So I went back to bed and didn't sleep, but waited for
Alex to tell me in the morning.

The next day, Alex told me why he had woken up
screaming in his bed.

He said in the night a boy called 'Christopher' had come to him, he was a ghost, and he seemed to have slight learning difficulties. He was an albino. He had told Alex that he lived in a children's home and that the master of the house had killed him. As the boy had explained this to Alex, Alex said he had been taken out of his body and taken back in time to the old house into a big kitchen, and the master of the house was throwing Alex around the room across a big old kitchen table. Alex said the master was very well dressed in a suit but was very angry that the boy was telling him about himself.
Alex said the boy had told him that he was not to worry about Harvey, that he would out live us, and in return, would Alex be able to help him as he was stuck.

Well Alex doesn't make this sort of thing up. He was really shook up about it, but he hadn't wanted to tell me, as he new I was having trouble sleeping with the amount of pain I was in.
Harvey's health has been a constant worry for us. We were anxious that every time he was ill, this might be his end, so for the ghost 'Christopher' to tell Alex that Harvey was going to out live us was fantastic. Alex knew we had to help the boy, but we hadn't been religious, and didn't have a clue what we needed to do.

We had in the past watched a few 'Most Haunted' when Derek Acora was on it, and both been intrigued by what he would say, but like most people, was a bit sceptical about it. But now, we had hands on dealing with a ghost. Alex had seen and spoken to him and I had heard him call out to me, but I was too scared to accept it.

The holiday then got very challenging. We weren't getting any sleep, as negative feelings where happening all night. The children had a fantastic time. We had booked half board and the food was great, but Alex and I were so tired. I said to Alex, I'm going to ask reception if there is any history of the main house or any ghosts. Alex said they will think we're mad.
I plucked up the courage and asked. I said to the receptionist, "has there ever been any one mention a boy ghost before?"
She went quiet and said "just a minute." Then she went out the back.
When she came back, she had an A4 6 page print out of the history of the house, before it had been a holiday park. It had been built in the 1890's. She said " there's been no reports of a boy ghost, but there is a ghost Mary in the main house."
I thanked her and then we went back to our chalet and read the leaflet.
In it, it said that the house had been a children's home between 1930-1940's. It tallied with Christopher's story.

Alex was getting more concerned that the boy was a tortured soul, and needed help, so I text my friend Maria, who is a heavily religious Christian and I wrote:- This sounds funny, but Alex had a boy ghost come to him in the night, and he wants to help him move on!

Maria text back, but I never got the text. My phone deleted all my text messages and there was a red cross shown as the front screen. I could ring home to seen how the dogs were, but it didn't accept any incoming calls. Then, one morning we were going off to breakfast, and I couldn't find my hairbrush. When I came back from breakfast it had been placed in the middle of the double bed. It was not there when we had gone out. Alex said to me "Christopher wants to help you, he put it there." Harvey was very aware Christopher was around. He played with his invisible friend as much as he could. One night we came back from the disco, it was a bright starry night, and everyone had gone in except Harvey and me. Harvey didn't want to go in. So I sat on a bench and watched him playing with his invisible friend for 45 minutes, until I got too cold. Harvey really was happy. The next day I told Mum and Patrick what had been happening with us. I knew she wouldn't believe me. She just mocked me. When we were telling Patrick about my phone , he looked at his phone, and there was a weird picture on it like a UFO. He didn't understand where it had come from. Patrick did believe us.

There was only one message left in my inbox on my phone, which was the only picture message I had saved. I didn't think to look at it, but thinking back I am grateful I didn't as if the bad ghost had barred my phone, I hate to think what he had done to the image on my phone.

We managed to stay the week. It was hard, as by Wednesday I just wanted to go home, I was petrified if the bad ghost that had killed Christopher might hurt Alex. But the children would have been mortified if we had gone home early.

I had taken a fancy dress outfit for Evie and Harvey, as usually there is a fancy dress competition on these types of holidays. I used to be the mum that would make them, but now with Harvey, I don't get the time. Unfortunately the outfit I had brought for Harvey was a devil costume he had had for Halloween. It had been hanging in the cupboard in the children's bedroom, and there was no doors on the cupboard. As the week went on, my oldest son Myles seemed to get unwell, feeling sick and started to become very angry and said bad things. It was as if he was being controlled by something bad.

Evie was saying, "Harvey's going to wear his devils outfit, I think the devil lives in hell."

Myles snapped at her "There's no such place as hell, hell is when you cant move on!"

I looked at him and said, "what did you just say?"

He said," I don't know, did I say something?"

It was as if the bad ghost had spoken through him.

The morning we left the Holiday park, Evie and Harvey were very sad. Harvey had collected some pebbles and shells from the beach. He got some from out of his bag, and placed them in the bed side draw of the double bed where he had been sleeping. He did the sign for friend. I said to him, "Are they for Christopher?" he signed "yes". I left those shells and pebbles in the draw. Alex said the next people that stayed in the chalet would probably get pelted by them in the night.

As we drove away from the Holiday site, and we were about a mile away, I looked at my phone and the red cross disappeared and all my old Inbox messages returned. It was as if the negative spirit couldn't effect it this far away.

When we got back, Alex told his mum and dad about what had happened. It had really shaken us. They did believe Alex, and they asked Alex's aunties friend who is a medium, if she could help Christopher on to a better place. We were told later that Christopher had moved on with 5 others who had also died like him. Still to this day that news makes my skin crawl. I had told myself the master had lost his temper with Christopher and it had been a mistake, but hearing that other boys had died in the same way, made me really upset. Had I known that while we were on holiday, I would definitely have come home earlier.

# Meeting a Healer

We have noticed every time when ever we have been away as a family, the night we return, Harvey gets very vocal when putting him to bed. Almost as if chatting to all the spirits in his bedroom that have missed him.

As the summer went on, my back pain got worse, and I asked the doctor for more pain relief. The pediatrician at hospital had prescribed amitriptyline in a small dose, which she said worked well on the nervous system. But in larger doses it acts as an antidepressant. I had said no to this, as I am a strong person and I know how these types of drugs become addictive. Having suffered from anorexia and bulimia from the age of 15 to 20, I never wanted to be addicted to anything again. But I really couldn't cope with the pain anymore, so I gave it a go. This did work really well, but made me really drowsy, and I hated having no zip!

Harvey's 1 To 1, Jacky, at school, had been telling me about a lady she had been seeing that did natural healing. Jacky had been poorly and was just getting over a stomach operation. The lady 'Harriet' had given her a treatment and Jacky had come back glowing.

After the Holiday experience we had just had, I started to wonder if I should make an appointment to see Harriet. Its something I never imagined I would ever do, but I made an appointment. I didn't want to be on happy pills for the rest of my life.

A couple of days before I visited Harriet, I was lying in bed. The pain killers had all worn off and it was about 3am. I was lying with one leg over hanging the edge of the bed.  It was impossible to get into a position that wasn't excruciating. The pain was immense. I started to cry, and shake a little bit, but I was trying really hard not to, as I didn't want to  wake anyone. Lying there I was thinking, "I can't cope with this much pain, but if I die now, who will look after the children?"
Then I thought about Harvey seeing angels, and all the other downs syndrome children seeing them. So I thought,  "Right, angels if your there, and you come and help Harvey, can you help me now, and take my pain away?"
Well about 1 minute later, the pain totally went, completely and utterly!!! I was amazed. In my head I was saying, "thank you so much angels."
This worked for about four hours, and then the pain would come flooding back. I asked again and it worked.

The day I met Harriet, I walked into her treatment room, she had a lovely bubbly smile and a very warm welcome. She sat me down. My appointment was for 4 o'clock. She was younger than me at 28.

We chatted and I poured out my history of back pain, Harvey, and how the angels had been helping. She listened and chatted about how she had always been pestered by spirits, but now she worked only with love and light, how her life had changed.

There was a lot more to it than that, but I had to pinch myself as this all felt like I was watching something on the telly, but this was really happening. She asked me to lie on the bed. I laid on my front, as I couldn't lay on my back. She placed her hands on me and gave me a Reki treatment. (It was really hard for me not to giggle, as I felt a bit self conscious).

She also handed me a book to take home and read, it was Louise Hays 'You Can Heal Your Life',. This made me feel great, as she had never met me before, and yet she trusted me to bring back her book. This book is a must have.

Afterwards we chatted some more. When I went to leave she said, "Just one thing I've been trying to ask you all night. God wants to know why you are asking the angels for help and not him!"

I said, I have only got as far as the angels, because my son had told me about them, and they have helped me.

It was 7.30pm now and dark. I drove home, which is about 7 miles. As I drove, there was white sparks of light in front of my car going off like fireworks. I felt amazing. My back pain was just now a dull ache, and I couldn't explain or understand what the magic sparks were all about, I felt jubilant.

When I got home, Alex could see all the pain had come out of my face. I stopped taking the pain killers the next day. I haven't taken pain killers for my back since.

# Alex Gone Fishing

After leaving Harriet, I told Alex what she had said about asking God for help, and not just the angels. Alex found this a step too far, as he has always been of the mind set, that if there was a God, why would he let innocent children like Harvey suffer.

When you go to school, the primary School preach religion, and then you go to secondary, and they teach you that religion has been brought in to control the masses!

So when Alex went fishing the following Sunday, I thought I'd try a little experiment.

Alex had left the house at 6am. So both Harvey and Evie had woken up and got in bed with me. (Myles is a teenager now so this is the last place he would want to be!).

Evie asked where daddy had gone. I explained he had gone fishing and that I was going to pray to God for Daddy to catch a fish, but he must put it back and not bring it home. I new Alex would find this impossible, because the whole point of sea fishing is that you bring it home. Evie said she would pray to God as well.

When Alex came back at 11am, I asked how he got on. He said, "You know full well how I got on!"
I said, "Why?"

He said, "Yes I did catch a large Bass (a type of fish), but for some reason I was told to put it back in my head, so I did!"

When I told him what Evie and I had done, he was quite taken back by it all, and so was I.
Even if it was just power of thought, we were both amazed.

# My Pre-Op

I had an appointment come through to have a steroid injection into my spine. The hospital had offered this treatment, it's the first thing they do with a herniated disc, before they operate on your spine. The epidural was supposed to relax the pain around the disc to give me 6 months pain relief. The human body is amazing, and in some cases, this has worked, but if it doesn't, I would then need to have an operation.

The week after seeing Harriet I went for my pre-op. I was a bit unsure now. Two weeks before I was desperate for this injection, now, I felt much better after Harriet's treatment, but it had taken over a year to get this treatment sorted out, and what if my back pain suddenly increased.

The day of the pre-op, they weighed me, but did not take my blood, and I was booked in for the following week. Afterwards we went to the shops, as I wanted to get some nice paper to make some party invites for my 40th birthday. We went into W H Smiths, and at the end of an isle, there was a magazine, with a book and a dvd, that had been reduced down from £14.99 to £2. It seemed to glow bright around the edges. I looked at Alex and Alex looked at me. I said, "Did you see that?"
He said, "Yes."

We walked closer and it was a book entitled 'Angels'.
I said to Alex, "Should we buy it then?" and he replied, "I
think we should."

I paid for it at the checkout feeling a bit embarrassed
that I was buying an angel book. My Mum would not be
impressed. The Lady behind the till gave me a free
'Times' newspaper for some reason as well. It was all a bit
surreal.

That night I sat in bed with Alex watching 'Sarah
Beanies' House Restoration, which I love, as I am an
Architectural technician, but have lost touch since having
the children.
I said to Alex, I might get Harvey's DVD player and
watch that angel DVD while this is on, just out of
interest.
Alex had the laptop on his lap, writing a letter to
someone that had not paid their bill.
As the angel DVD played I thought this is just going to
be about trying to sell me crystals and that sort of
gimmick. Then it got to the point where your supposed to
meditate. It was saying, "Your sitting on a bench in a
beautiful garden with your angel, she is now going to tell
you her name."
I was still watching Sarah Beanie at the same time, and
thinking, "Yer what ever."

Then I said to Alex "Do you know anyone called Fiona, or Fleur?"

He looked at me and said, "No."

The next day I rang Harriet up to ask what to do about the epidural. I said I'm booked in next week. She said, "Can't you put it off for a couple of months, and see if the Reiki works?"

She could also offer acupuncture, reflexology and Sports Massage.

I said I had been waiting so long and didn't want to start all over again with the NHS.

I then told her about the angel DVD, and I think my angel is called Fiona. She said, "There is an angel card called Fiona, I will email you the reading on the card. If your not meant to have the epidural there will be a sign."

The DVD also said that angels sometimes leave a sign by way of a white feather to show they are near. I thought this was a pile of slushy nonsense before Harriet told me that there is an angel card called Fiona.

I have never seen angel cards before. Apparently Fiona is the angel that welcomes you into the angel realms, on the card there is a picture of her with her arms out beckoning you in.

I waited for Harriet to send me the Fiona reading, It came 2 days later. It tallied and told me that the angels have tried to help me all my life, but I had blocked them, and to ask for help when ever I want. As I was reading it a tear ran down my face, and then my daughters ZuZu toy hamster that was on the bedroom floor said, "Are you alright Claire?"
I ran out of the room traumatized!

# I Get A Sign

The night before my epidural was due, I still was unsure
whether to go ahead with it or not. My back pain was
reducing, but all the anxiety of not knowing if I should go
or not was niggling it.

During the night, Harvey always wakes up, and when he
realizes there is no one next to him, he usually comes into
our bed, and I get out and go into his bed. I hadn't really
slept. As I walked into his room his Buzz Lightyear toy
went off, and I hadn't even touched it. I picked it up and
put it in another bedroom. I thought, was that the sign I
needed not to go to hospital in the morning?

When morning came, I had a shower and every one had
left the bedroom. When I came back into the bedroom,
there was a white feather on the floor. That was my sign.
I rang the hospital immediately, and cancelled my
epidural. I told them I had diarrhea, which wasn't a lie, I
had panic bum!

When I went back to Harriet's, I explained what had
happened, and she told me that when she had sent me the
email of angel Fiona, she also had 3 other readings. One
was angel Opal, who after reading the card, explains that
she watches over Harvey, then the card compassion, and
the other card was that I was a natural healer.

I didn't doubt this because since I had been asking the angels to take my back pain away, I had also been kissing Harvey's eyes and asked the angels to keep them clear, as he has always suffered dreadfully with conjunctivitis. This has worked, and we haven't had to put drops in his eyes or clean them since. We used to do this morning and night.

I started to pray every day to thank god and the angels for making my back pain better and for helping keep Harvey well and his eyes and ears clear.

# EFT

My friend Maria, who I explained earlier is heavily religious, has a grandson with downs syndrome, and as her daughter died, she is bringing him up. He is the same age as Harvey, but doesn't have hearing or speech difficulties and has not been as poorly as Harvey.

We went on an outing together, and she brought her friend along. Her friend Pat is Reiki trained, but also was promoting the use of EFT. So she kindly sent me an email on EFT, which she advised me to watch. She proclaimed it would help my back along side the Reiki.

I sat and watched it for 20 minutes, and sort of tailored it to suit my needs. So now I do the eft which takes me about a minute every day, and works really well for me as a pain reducer. You have to tap on pressure points on your arms, face, neck and upper body, which releases signals to your brain to eliminate pain. This is much more scientific than Reiki, so I talk to my mum about this.

# Taking my First Degree Reiki

When I went back to Harriet, on my third visit, I asked if she thought I was ready to be Reiki trained, and if she knew anyone who could train me. I said the angels are working really well with my back pain and Harvey at the minute, but if I could offer Harvey Reiki as well it would be amazing.
Since Harvey was born, I have always said to Alex, all the money in the world couldn't give me what I want, and that's for Harvey to be well!

Harriet explained that being a Reiki Master, she could train me for Reiki, so we agreed a date in December, (probably not the best time of year to do it looking back with hindsight).

I didn't realize what you go through when you are Reiki tuned. It was life changing. The week before during the night I kept hearing footsteps, but when I opened the door to the bedroom, no one was there. The day of the attunement was a lovely day, and surprisingly there was a fair bit to read. She said there might be some side effects, but I dismissed this.

OMG, my nose didn't stop running for days, then I couldn't sleep at night. I would lie their just thinking I must go round and see my Dad, as he was really poorly, and I might be able to help. Then their was my mums friend with a bad back, then there.......... the list goes on. But obviously looking back, the world isn't ready for me yet and I don't need my straight jacket just yet!

I did go round and give my dad a Reiki treatment. Something I never imagined I would say! My dad is like my Mum in that they believe;- you live, you die, end of!! My parents are separated now.
My Dad was really ill, and I had to do something. He had been waiting 18 months for a knee operation, as a cow had stood on his knee and shattered it, and apparently that is not classed in A&E as an emergency. The pain had been getting to him and he had picked up a flue bug as well. He had seen me a couple of months ago in a lot of pain my self, and I had told him that I had been receiving Reiki treatment and he should give it a go.

I left home the morning after I had been Reiki tuned to visit my dad. I had prayed to the angels and God to help me with my first Reiki treatment for my dad. As I left my house a large rainbow appeared with all the colours of the rainbow as clear as clear. My dad lives 17 miles away from me, but that rainbow followed me all the way to his house, so I felt the help was with me. The colours of the rainbow are how the Chakras are present in the human body. Chakras are something new to me.

My dad was a complete wreck before the treatment, but when I rang him the following week, he was talking about doing some building work!

When I had been Reiki tuned for about 3 days, I hadn't slept, and my cold had got worse. I rang Harriet. She said I must close down my third eye, my psyche., because I'm not shutting down at the minute, and its important to know when to ask for Reiki. It took me a while to sort this one out.

I Reiki Harvey every night when we go to bed now, and it sends him to sleep. If he has trouble switching off in the night, I put my hands on him and he goes to sleep almost instantly. This is amazing, as we all get a lot more sleep than we used to, no more telly tubbies at 4 am when he can't sleep!

# Four leaf Clovers

I carried on visiting Harriet for Reiki treatments on a monthly basis, and during one of my reiki treatments I had a feeling that someone or thing was pinching my cheeks. Then the name Ken popped into my head. So I said to Harriet, "Do you know anyone called Ken? The only one I know is Ken Barlow!"
Apart from angels names I get now and then, I haven't had this happened before. She couldn't think of anyone called Ken. That evening she text me, and said, "My grandad used to be called Ken, and he pinched my checks!"
I was really chuffed.

I still felt that the Reiki treatment Harriet was giving me seemed to last longer than mine, so she suggested that I took my Reiki Second Degree.
The day before I did this I was out walking the dogs, and I found 8 four leaf clovers. I knew that tomorrow was going to be a good day. I find four leaf clovers a lot, and it usually happens the day before something good happens. The week before I met Harriet I found 18!

During the day of my Reiki Two, I was telling Harriet that I had found 8 four leaf clovers, and she said, "That's great, I have never found a four leaf clover, and I would love to have one".
We didn't realize the relevance of them, we both just knew they were lucky.

We left the room and then Harriet locked the door, and she didn't go back for a few days. But when she did, on the floor in front of her was a perfectly pressed four leaf clover. No one had entered that room, it was as if all the spirits had been listening to us  and given Harriet a present.
After googling, I have found out that the four leaf clover in Christianity signifies Love, Hope, Luck, and Faith. There is 1 four leaf clover to every 10,000 three leaf clover. I still keep finding them, so I feel very lucky.
I even thought I needed to start going to church, so I went to my local Chapel, along with my daughter Evie, thinking I can do this, right up until the minister asked the congregation to sign a petition against same sex marriages. This totally shook me, as I believe god loves anyone who gives and receives love, this can only be a good thing, irrelevant of who they love.  So I wont be going back.

# Harvey's Friend.

I asked Harriet if she knew anyone who could tell me what or who Harvey is playing with, and she gave me the contact details of her friend Rachael who is a medium, so I contacted her.

She drew me a picture of Harvey's Spirit Guide 'Nathaniel', and she explained to me how his guide had helped us on this path of discovery to find Reiki, to help Harvey and all of us as a Family.

When I showed Harvey the spirit guide picture and asked him who it was, he signed to me, it was his friend.

## Harvey's Spirit Guide 'Nathaniel'

# A Year On.

I have struggled with Harvey and have a loving Husband, but we don't have any family help, as my sisters and grandparents have all backed away.

The only help I get is through paid 1 to 1. The one lady who has helped more than her share needs to be mentioned, and that is Vikki. We originally met her as Harvey's swimming coach, but she is also a school teacher and she is amazing with special needs children. She loves Harvey and Evie, and they love her. She is like a young version of me. She has a spinal curvature, which can be very painful at times, but my Reiki works for her, and she has been there while I have been going though this process of discovery, so she accepts my help, even if she thinks I'm a little weird!

Harvey's Passion is swimming, and I have embraced this, to the point where he is a confident swimmer. Taking him swimming used to be the only break for me, as when in the water with him, he would be content and focused. Usually he would be seeking the next activity, or trying to run off. His mind seemed to be over active, but once in the water, he would relax and enjoy it. Afterwards he would be more settled for the rest of the day, which was much more enjoyable.

I have read news paper articles about the Downs Syndrome International Swimming Organization, and hope to build up Harvey's fitness so he can compete when he's older. These championships are held all over the world.

It is amazing how thought has such a power. As human beings we overlook this, but every single thing you think does have an effect on the universe.

I no longer block the angels, whenever I get into an awkward situation, I simply think, right angels, can you help? Before you know it the situation is resolved. Only this morning, Harvey would not let me dress him for school. So I asked for help. Suddenly I had an idea to persuade him, and he suddenly became very co-operative. Persuasion does not usually work, as his lack of understanding prevents it, but he has come on amazingly well in the last 12 months.

Recently Harvey's Doctor asked us to make an appointment to see her. He is on repeat prescription medicine for asthma. She hadn't seen him for a year and it is policy to review this annually. Until this last year we were constantly visiting the doctors as he was always so unwell, so we have never needed to do this before!

I have spent my whole life doubting myself, and know I don't have too. I know what's happened to me is a lot to take on board, but it has been better than winning the lottery.

Harvey still has Downs Syndrome and behavior difficulties, but by keeping him well, he is getting more opportunities to learn, and in turn his development is progressing. He brings so much happiness to everyone. I now can say I have a happy **healthy** family!

# How Can You Change Your Life Now.

If you still think ok, "so how is all this relevant to me, never having any beliefs or religion." Where do I start? I would recommend you try to get a moment to yourself. I know this is very hard, caring for a special needs child is mentally draining, and time is so precious when you get it to yourself. There are always mountains of jobs to be done. If you do get a window of opportunity, just sit or relax calmly, and try to clear your mind of any thoughts. Simply ask for angel help. You may be surprised with the outcome. I find when I first wake up I'm most relaxed. You can also ask when you are struggling and need help, you don't have to speak out load, as everyone around will think you have gone mad. Just simply think, "please angels, can you help me now?"

You just need the intention to allow the energy to work with you. Be aware and open to follow your instincts.

Even though you are exhausted, it is basic common sense that it will help to treat people as you yourself would like to be treated, and try to remain positive at all times.

What ever your belief you have or haven't got, give Reiki a go. Reiki means 'universal life force', in Japanese. The Rei being 'universal' and the ki being 'life force', helping to heal each individuals needs. It can only produce a positive result, even if its just that you managed to relax and unwind for a while.

Trust me, Harvey has introduced me to angels, and Harriet has introduced me to Reiki, but they both have given me a leap of faith, and its transformed my life.

Good Luck on your journey!